ALL ABOUT
Debugging Code

BY MEG MARQUARDT

The Child's World®
childsworld.com

Published by The Child's World®
1980 Lookout Drive • Mankato, MN 56003-1705
800-599-READ • www.childsworld.com

Photographs ©: Shutterstock Images, cover,
1, 5, 6, 9, 24; Shot Prime Studio/Shutterstock
Images, 13; Jacob Lund/Shutterstock Images,
14; Kent Weakley/Shutterstock Images, 17;
Blue Planet Studio/Shutterstock Images, 18

ISBN 9781503832015
LCCN 2018962803

Printed in the United States of America
PA02418

ABOUT THE AUTHOR

Meg Marquardt has been gaming since she was a little girl. Today, she loves to research and write about game design, E-Sport competitions, and more. She lives in Madison, Wisconsin, with her two scientist cats, Lagrange and Doppler.

TABLE OF CONTENTS

CHAPTER 1

Bug Hunt

Lena is excited to play her new computer game. Lena hits the left arrow, and her character walks backward. She hits the up arrow, and it jumps. Then Lena hits the right arrow on her keyboard. Nothing happens.

Lena asks her mom for help. They look at the keyboard. The right arrow key will not press down. Lena and her mom carefully pull the key off the keyboard. A small beetle is stuck under the key! The bug is stopping the character from moving forward. Once Lena and her mom remove it, the right arrow key works. Now the character can move normally.

The bug in the keyboard made Lena's game not work correctly.

All coders have to deal with bugs. So they must learn how to fix them.

6

Debugging computer **code** is just like finding a real bug in a machine. Code is written instructions that a computer follows to run programs. If there is a problem with the code, the computer will not work correctly. The problem is often called a **bug**. Even the best **coders** run into bugs. It takes practice to learn how to spot a problem in code. Debugging is one of the most important skills a coder can have.

CHAPTER 2

What Is a Coding Bug?

A coder is designing a computer game. He wants the character on the screen to jump when he hits the space bar. Instead, the character ducks when he hits the space bar. This problem is a coding bug.

A bug is different from a coding **error**. An error in the code means that the program cannot work at all. But with a bug, the program will still run. It just will not do what it was supposed to. In the computer game example, the character still moves. But it is supposed to jump instead of duck.

Errors make programs stop working altogether.

9

A bug can be a wrong letter, word, or **symbol** in the code. A coder might type the letter *h* when she needs to type *d*. Bugs can also happen when code is missing important parts. For example, a coder might tell the computer to make a character cast a spell. But the coder might forget the line of code that gives the character magical powers. In that case, the computer knows it is supposed to tell the character to do something. But the computer is missing important information. When the computer runs the code to cast the spell, the character does not do anything. This is a problem that needs to be debugged.

Problems with code can be very small. These bugs are very hard to spot. A coder wants a computer to display "Hello, World!" on its screen. He types out the code. When he tests the code, it does not work correctly. The coder looks carefully at each character in the lines of code. Then he spots the bug. He forgot to type the * symbol. The coder adds the * symbol, and the code works.

Code with a Bug

```
program helloworld
print, "Hello, World!"
end program helloworld
```

Debugged Code

```
program helloworld
print*, "Hello, World!"
end program helloworld
```

CHAPTER 3

Debugging Code

Debugging is a skill that every coder must learn. No matter how talented coders are, they will have to deal with bugs.

Because debugging is a skill, practice can help coders get better at it. One way that coders try to spot bugs is to test their code often. A big program might have hundreds or thousands of lines. Code can be full of bugs if a coder waits until the very end of writing her code to test it. Testing code bit by bit helps catch bugs earlier in the process and saves time.

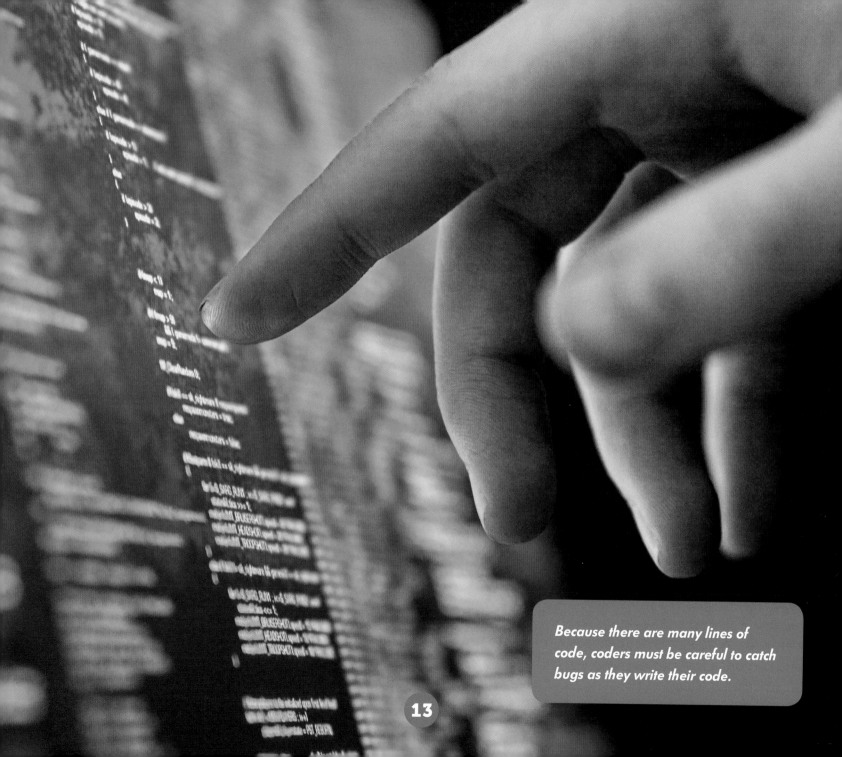

Because there are many lines of code, coders must be careful to catch bugs as they write their code.

13

Coders often need to work together to fix bugs.

Even with testing, some bugs might slip through. When faced with bugs, coders can take steps to fix them. Coders can first check the **stack trace**. A stack trace shows what the computer was doing when it hit a bug in the code. This helps the coders know where to look in the code to find the bug. Once they know where to look, coders can try to fix the bug. As they work, they can run more tests on only the part of the code that has the bug.

Sometimes coders cannot fix the bug on their own. There are websites where coders can post their problems and get help from other coders. Debugging code is often a group effort.

CHAPTER 4

Bugs in the Real World

Coders do not always catch bugs before it is too late. When bugs are missed, bad things can happen.

For example, things headed to space have blown up because of bugs in code. In 1962, a missing hyphen caused a machine heading to Venus to go off course. Because the course could not be corrected, the machine had to be blown up just five minutes after it took off. An even bigger accident happened in 1996. A European rocket had a bug that caused all systems on board to crash. The rocket exploded just 40 seconds after it took off.

Rockets rely on computer code. Bugs can cause failed take-offs and even explosions.

Bugs in programs that buy and sell parts of companies can lose a lot of money.

18

Bugs can also cost people a lot of money. Bugs in programs that buy and sell things can cost hundreds of millions of dollars. In 2012, Knight Capital Company used a faulty **algorithm**. An algorithm is a program that takes a lot of data and makes choices. This algorithm made choices about buying and selling parts of companies. The bug caused the algorithm to make many bad choices. It lost the company $440 million in just 30 minutes before it was shut down.

Bugs can cause big problems. That is why coders have to be good at spotting and fixing them. With practice and with the help of others, coders can squash any bug in their code.

Q: What is a bug?

A: A bug is a problem in a line of code.

Q: How is a bug different from an error?

   a. A program can still run with an error. A program cannot run with a bug.

   b. A program can still run with a bug. A program cannot run with an error.

   c. It is not different. Bugs and errors are the same.

A: b. A program can still run with a bug. A program cannot run with an error.

Q: What is fixing a bug called?

      a. squashing

      b. debugging

      c. running

      d. mending

A: b. debugging

Q: What should coders do if they cannot figure out how to fix a bug on their own?

A: Coders should ask other coders for help.

GLOSSARY

algorithm (AL-go-ri-them) An algorithm is a program that makes choices based on data. The algorithm chose what to buy.

bug (BUG) A bug makes computer code not work right. A bug in the computer game's code made the character duck instead of jump.

code (KOHD) Code is a list of instructions that computers follow to do things. The code made the character in the computer game jump.

coders (KOHD-urz) Coders are people who write code. Coders create computer games.

debugging (dee-BUG-ing) Debugging is the action of removing problems in code. Debugging code is an important skill for coders.

error (ER-ur) An error in code keeps a program from working at all. The error made it so that the program would not run.

stack trace (STAK TRAYSS) A stack trace shows what the computer was doing when it hit a bug in the code. A coder can check the stack trace to find a bug.

symbol (SIM-bul) A symbol is a character on the keyboard that is not a number or letter. The coder forgot to put the * symbol in his code.

IN THE LIBRARY

Harris, Patricia. *Understanding Coding through Debugging*. New York, NY: PowerKids Press, 2017.

Scott, Marc. *A Beginner's Guide to Coding*. New York, NY: Bloomsbury, 2017.

Wood, Kevin. *Get Coding with Debugging*. New York, NY: Rosen Publishing, 2018.

ON THE WEB

Visit our website for links about coding:
childsworld.com/links

Note to Parents, Teachers, and Librarians: We routinely verify our
Web links to make sure they are safe and active sites.
So encourage your readers to check them out!

INDEX